Pick a

Garnet to

Sleep in

Also by Kim Shuck

Smuggling Cherokee
Rabbit Stories
Clouds Running in
Sidewalk Ndn
Murdered Missing
Deer Trails
Whose Water
Exile Heart
What Unseen Thing Blows Wishes Across My Surface
Noodle, Rant, Tangent

Anthologies edited/co-edited

Words Upon the Waters (Karla Brundage, Sara Biel, &
        Kim Shuck, Eds.)
Oakland Out Loud (Karla Brundage & Kim Shuck, Eds.)
The City Is Already Speaking, vols. 1-4 (Thea Matthews, Kim
        Shuck, & Denise Sullivan, Eds.)
Beat Not Beat (Rich Fergusson, S.A. Griffen, Alexis
        Rhone-Fancher, & Kim Shuck, Eds.)
This Wandering State
Home in the Bay (Emma Rosenbaum & Kim Shuck, Eds.)

Pick a Garnet to Sleep in

poems

KIM SHUCK

Scapegoat Press
Kansas City, Missouri

Cover Photo and author photo by Douglas A. Salin
        www.dougsalin.com
Cover art by Kim Shuck

ISBN 978-0-971291-8-6

Scapegoat Press
P.O. Box 410962
Kansas City, Missouri 64141

scapegoatpress.com

"Hunting in the Downtown" previously appeared in the
anthology *Home in the Bay*, edited by Kim Shuck and Emma
Rosenbaum (Aunt Lute Books).

Contents

(Poems without titles are listed by first line)

I

II

III

IV

For everyone who has been derailed by plague, fire, infestation, famine and genocidal actions. I hope to see you on the other side.

They've mistaken my bones again
Standing at the site of excavation
Surrounded by the white clad
The masked
In the hearing rooms
The hours long
Uncut
Testimony

The tooth drilled for testing
The bones are mine alright
Femur
Curled like a fern frond
I cradle it like a doll
Sing the old songs
So it will know me
Like so many others I collect
Rewire
Begin all of our stories again

Wounds are not a good compass but
Sometimes
Our tools are numb
Another poet slips away
The demon in the skyline is being renamed
An exorcism
A costume
We follow our own blood trails in
Dazed mathematics
Another poet passes
We chase puzzles
Already decoded
Tell ourselves outdated answers like
Children wanting
Bedtime stories
Wanting
A stuffed animal shaped like an equestrian statue
Because there are heroes
Because there must be heroes
Singing the words of poets who have left us
In this time of necromancy
This time of the mazed
The smell of our own blood
On these sidewalks

Blood and easily overlooked
Chamomile
A possibility
Anywhere the pavement breaks

Chimeric identity
Difficult to see whole
The seams the
Tragedies
The super models
Mystical difference
If you need to hear it
I'll say it now
You exist
I've seen you
Heard your chosen name
Being human is a risk
Dancing conscious
Life maps are legacy furniture
Psychological footstools you can
Store or reject
Self a thing that has to be taken
New
Each time
With whatever clumsy grace
Can be found in the day

Spin
How can you watch yourself
Healing
Over and over and
Think yourself weak?
Not everyone has to invent or
Excavate
Words for self
Word at the base of the throat
The timbre of voice
Word from tattered paper mache
Sarcophagus
Flesh consumed and
Literally buried
Rediscovered
Word from
Self from self
You are surrounded
But not alone
I press my cheek
Against the stone
And sing an old song
An old song
That someone else once
Carefully
Reassembled

We meet online to read to one another
Three more people I love test positive
We close the door we
Close
And even here in this shiny
In this firework and
This year will be
There is already a completion
My emotions have been on vacation for months
Bad news is
Oh
Good news is
Oh ok
I rattle self
Rattle
To hear what might be in here with me

I plan to ask the children if they've ever been heartbroken
Terrified
Felt anything so overwhelming that the
Feeling changed them
Maybe in the cells
Maybe in the DNA
What is the next step?
The step you take into the change?
What has shaken you?
Don't answer
The answer will make you vulnerable
And we live in a something like a walls down asylum
Something old fashioned with ice baths
And questionable mandatory surgery
Any unprotected person could find themselves
Strapped to a bed
In a ward
Trapped in expectation
You are only protected if you conform
The rules for fitting in change in each city block
It takes constant vigilance
I plan to ask the children
If they've ever lost anything precious to them
Maybe something they didn't treat as well as they might have
The beloved doll

Dragged by one foot or
A book read to pieces
That door to some other idea
That door can come apart in your hands
Don't answer
Loss makes you look weak
Weakness is considered a wound
The predators will come to feed
I want to ask them how they moved past the loss
Was it possible to move past the loss?
Was it possible to move past the guilt?
Don't answer
Guilt is an admission of unworthiness
I'm going to spoil the suspense
Everyone may be found unworthy at any time
You can't have control of that
You own thoughts will follow you
What will you do to open a door?
What will be behind the door?
Is the door your private door?
Will you let your fears make you fearless?
Don't answer
Make plans
Maybe I'll see you again
Good luck

Which headstones are these?
Misplaced trust
We are,
She says,
A nation of laws
Laws that set limits at the extremes
That define the edges not the heart
And every new report makes clear what is protected
That the plea
Don't kill us
Is a bigger threat than a stew of
Guns and misogyny
That our prayers are met with violence
The way that racism can't see racism
The way that deadly cosplay
Stands in for heroism
Because some other guys did it before
Some other time
In defense of a thought
We can't even hire people to defend these days
Are presented with terrorism selfies
And a song we already know

Tongue Tied

*This one is dedicated to Nazelah Jamison; it has roots in the
list of words forbidden to the CDC by the 45th president of the
United States and scraps of thought from a lifetime of being told
that it is not our turn to be free yet.*

Surprise is not a condition of heartbreak
Captive tongue
Strangled thought
Breath
The breath leads the word and sometimes
The word leads the breath
I can't breathe and
I am not surprised
The daily walk over word shards
Left by
Bullies off the leash and hunting
Leaves me limping
We are dying
We
Are dying
Mouths choked with forbidden words
Disallowed
Unspoken
Diversity will now only refer to the variety of ways

in which we can be
Murdered
By people who are in charge
A woman beaten is a woman beaten
Made to breathe the shatter of belief at the hands
of authorities
The ones who write the rules
The breath leads the word
Sometimes the word leads the breath
Sometimes
I can't breathe
And some are left vulnerable
A word we will now only use to mean the feelings
of someone in charge
Feelings that must be wrapped in hoped for reflections
of power and control
Our voices hostage
I am not surprised
The breath leads the word
The breath leads a truth
Not an alternative
A truth
And the dictionaries are rewritten by bullies
Off the leash and hunting

They are entitled
A word we will now use to mean the rights of some to strip
the rights of others
We used to use other words for that
            but words have changed
As the old dictionaries
Grow into banned books
Grow as the list of banned words
Banned ideas
Grows
I'm not surprised
As more people are rendered

Speechless

As the hundreds of years of
        rumor of our death
Is enforced
We are said to have vanished
        so we vanish
And those who declare
        themselves allies
Identify the priorities for us
I am not surprised
That our safety is still not on
        that list
And if I am silenced by law or
        by a man
Who overtalks me for having an
        answer he feels is wrong
In a time where we need to
        demonstrate unity
In yet another time where the
        word "we" will be defined by
        someone else
I am not surprised
But I can still be heartbroken

I find it hard to breathe
And the breath leads the word
And I am weary
And I am not yet beaten
And make no mistake
Not everyone has been silenced

Tracking myself

I'm clever it's hard to find the traces
Online
Outline
Punctuated with death conversations
With people I barely know
And would probably like
Or love
Or compete with
In some other narrative
Poems I have no memory of
Trading card cousins
Finally the dearly held anger
Scars from over forty years ago
"Show me on the picture
The places you won't let heal"

We find the spill pile of dirt under the front stairs
Think of friends as
Portraits in place
Stored behind panes of glass
Houses as china cabinets
The next empathy disorder
Revealed and mocked on social media
Street cat
Stares intently at the front yard
Evidence
The lights in the other windows
Evidence
More evidence
China cabinet
Where grandma stored the ceremonial equipment
The friends sheltering still
Occluded portraits
Saved
For a coming celebration
Wishing Star
Hey cousin
I'm hearing more about you now
Than I ever did
I wonder

If everyone who will miss you
Will even know
What that sometime ache
Is tied to

Morning tastes of roasted peppernuts
A west coast prayer
Counting the dead
Mourning the
Dead
Fleeing fires
Setting fire
Afire
Fleeing gunfire
Out my window
Grey grace
Smoke
Shivers
Blooms
Another local mouthful
Here
In the sacred places

We aren't obligated to believe in each other
And it seems that for varying values of *we*
We don't
As D.C. waddles along counting other things
What a story
To be held up by symbols that you pull and chip
I have sketched them on my hands
When I can't think of what to write
Symbols from the edges of a story in progress
That believes I'm part of the prequel
That believes
For varying values of *they*
That for purposes of cosmetic surgery
We
Are best left symbolic
In movies and
Romantic art
In abstracted images of lithic suffering
But not
Dancing in ceremony
In celebration
Not
At the election
Not

Picking extreme numbers of backyard plums
And trying to give them away
But
Vanishing in law
Vanishing in cities
Vanishing by design

On Thursday I wear
Sapphires and lithium
Bridges from
Wednesday to morning song
We wake in the hour of grief
We wrap ourselves in overthink
And the lost and heroic
And the fragments of healing they might be
Pen tracks or
Unresolved chordings
They might be
Promise shards
Or other dangerous poisons
Might be a house sparrow
Perching on a fern tree
Might be the moth atlas
Another unfamiliar navigation
On Thursday
Day to conjure deep luck
To conjure restoration
Wrapped in warm
In language of edges
Sitting in among the lavender plants
And other sorts of poems

Mourning in 2020
I have too much time to think
I can't think
I
Push beads around push
Words around
Am late for everything
Distracted
Detached
The worst cuts
Are self-inflicted
I ran across one of your poems
today Stephen
And now I'm useless
Weighted down
By the things I miss

They're still painting the city all of the colors of
      an above-ground cemetery
Grey and grey
Veined white
A door like a flower against a headstone
Even though they're running
Running to somewhere else as was foretold
Repainting the house before they go
Touch up on the
Charcoal face
A door like a flower
With a heavy head
Stem bent
Wishing water
A house like a crypt
Dark
The next one marble white
And here in the pandemic
What do we know about how this crisis will run?
The people up the hill
The ones who smoke in the dark
In the night
Cigarette tip a flower
Blazing breath

I watch them
Don't think that they can see me
More than computer light
We sing our rituals in the dark
As some of the neighbor houses
Dark in recent days
For sale signs blooming like
Flowers for the dead
Flowers against a headstone

Distanced

We are 6 feet apart and masked
You are
As often
A self-folding model
You are
As often
Brittle looking
We don't hug
We are 8 feet apart
And masked
Walking
We don't hug
We are 1500 miles apart
In homes
Unmasked
You have no electricity
No water
Out of food
Remote
Touchless
Distanced

February or the month of bones of
Memories served in fine curls with breakfast with
Sundown
We crawl quietly into a love poem
I need you to live so that we can wrestle for the blankets
So that you can burn the coffee
So that my clutter can make you sigh
We wear our masks
On the outside
For another season

II

You can live through things you do not survive
The moment shakes me loose
The children
Still caged
Mercenaries
Black bagging protestors
I sing a song of Portland
Of Chicago and
Albuquerque
The threats to Oakland
Who will survive?
I paint my palms with the smell of prayer grass
And wonder what the power junkies are thinking
In the hole their addiction dug
What they believe will feed their sucking need for
Obedience
Control
Who will live?
Who survive?
We are hostage in a time of mercenaries
We are hostage
In a time of trouble
Tailored confusion
What are they thinking?
In their rooms

Not of destruction
But of indifference
And how will we find clean trouble
Clean trouble to stir like creek water
Trouble we will ask for an answer

I love the every direction power words spit cold into
        the face of this always storm
But can't afford the cry song
The next cry song
Something that curled up around the dust he kicked
        when he evoked us and then declared us
Gone
I'm not gone
The young man asked me if the rock I carry in my heart
The one handed over with a lineage back to initial invasion
The one with a chain attached that threads through
        continued occupation
The one that is hooked to every disappeared relative
Every murdered bone of every uninvestigated someone's child
Does your rock get too heavy Auntie?
Yes
It gets
Too
Heavy
Just now when someone who should be an ally declares us
Gone
In eloquent and delicious words and I think for a second that
Maybe we are but catch myself
My aging and practiced balance asserts itself and I remember

Nephew
The rock gets heavy and to carry it I have to cut
    other things away
So that you don't have to shoulder my share

What hour is this for a car to slip like a seal over the hill?
Lights cut at the window
Striking raindrop shadows
Sky creek
Finding level
Finding the echoes of Wounded Knee
Of the numbers we roll around in our symbols
Of the pen we can't find
Rattle of thinking
Rattle of mystery hours in a suspended time of year
Pendulum knocking over one more peg
Unwatched
Every year that image
Death by someone else's fear and the
Trailing connections of questions we think have been
      answered

How often the word *wall*?
Wall
Fact and scattered family
Scattered wall stone
Tumbled
Kitchen table revolution postponed
A stone
Not from a wall
One that fits the hand and
Once
I might have thrown it
I might have
But some windows are paper
Will not shatter will not
Shatter
Family
The web we cast between us
The school we make
The knots we tie
The numbers we decode
A revolution of soup
And acceptance

The Breaking

When they tore apart the sacred trees
Some of you are thinking of the Irminsul
Some are thinking cherry trees in front of
        the cultural center
Yes
I thought about every small thing destroyed
        to make a point
Now
I think about the petroglyphs
We saw them in the hot evening
There in the trees
Gone silent
And for now the memory of being there
Hidden
Near the state road
Is held by more than me
No less sacred
And after we who have seen are gone
In photos
And after the photos have faded
That story will be different
Like every missing woman
Like every grandma kicked to death

Like a bullet through
an apartment wall a
Legacy of breaking and
That story
Will be
Exactly the
Same
After all

Making a statement is not enough
But it is the very least
In a week of commentary
When will we have a week without commentary?
When the threat is accusation
Which somehow licenses some to silence the rest
Because their hurt feelings are the emergency
In a week of commentary
Who are marked and carry their crisis just everywhere?
Be angry
Get angry
The word is all shocked glass and the loudest voices
As philosophy debates
And insults
And accusations and
All of the words
And the callings out
There are eight bodies
And if this isn't your fight too
Whose fight is it?

As some politicians
Run voter equations
To decide who are people and who aren't
My African-American/Indigenous sister is run
through the algorithm
3/4 of 3/5 of a person
Just under a half
No human credit for the Indigenous fourth
        from a Nation not known to founders
My sons
Hawai`ian/Asian/European/Indigenous
Each a fourth of a person
Together half of a vote
Plus my half
Our little household worth one vote together
Leaving aside that the courts seem unwilling
        to support their actions
I'm not sure that these guys are up to the math.

Some prayers
Are small enough to fit in your mouth
Once released
Come together with other prayers
To quench a fire
A fire
A thing of disassembly
Your prayer
Small as thought
Small as fingerprint
That writes a lifetime
Just there
Just small
A mark
Not even a word
A mark
Part of a mark
Linking like chain
Like millions of prayers
Like poems
We will call it change
The personal is political
They said
And some of us were paying attention

But only for some people
A woman's movement that still doesn't
	speak to women of color
And other women
Because they will decide who is a woman and
Where reproductive rights ideology doesn't touch on those
Sterilized at the border
The personal is political
Unless it's a floor swept by someone not you
For less than minimum wage
The personal
Is political if it's your child dying
But not if it's someone indigenous vanished or murdered
Black lives
Caged children
Or a trans man on a barbed wire fence
I've heard that man say
The personal is political
But he only meant if he was that person

The People
Have been called this or that
This or that by tongues that couldn't say us
By politicians
Historians
Anthropologists
We are made small to fit in a shadow
A shadow
Made small
In boxes under a desk
The cast of my teeth
The professor asked for
Not a student but
Something else
Something else
The People
Blamed for ice age extinctions but
We haven't really been here very long?
We are thought of in pieces
We are thought of as history
We are defined out of existence
As something else

Today we are testing the idea of
representation
Blue dots on the sidewalk
Caravans stopping traffic
Bully politics
Voter intimidation
Today we are reviewing the experiment

Oppression Poem

Did my poem execute a no knock
Warrant on your address
In error?
Did it shoot you in your sleep?
Did the wild shots
From my poem
Fly through your neighbors' apartments
Endangering their lives?
Did my poem try to get your boyfriend to
Implicate you n your own death?
Did my poem
Suppress testimony that might
Make the poem look bad?
Is my poem
Still considered innocent
Of wrongdoing
In your shooting death?
Or did my poem make you feel bad?

Judged by our self-harm
The earlobe
The poison
The conversations with crows
Here we are
Tucked in under the drifting smoke
Make no mistake
Wood smoke
Dumpster smoke
Regular phone calls
Cry
Emergency
Emergency
House sparrows
Still
Fluff dust into their feathers
Near the neighbor's hedge
Here in a country with a nickname
A nickname that erases half of a planet
On a Wednesday morning
Spent spinning yarn out of time
And smoke
Remembering that Poe was found dead
After an election

This two block stretch is all
Tangential concrete and
Scattered remains of fireworks
Charred cardboard tubes that still smell of
Gunpowder and hormones
Some days I think I will write
Curses of self-awareness
Paint them on every sidewalk
In colors that only show in the presence of hubris
We could all use a little magic now and then
Maybe it doesn't have to taste of sarcasm
But don't we all navigate the world by poem?

Saturday fog
Is the true test of
Broken bells and
Friday night decisions
Dewslick stairs and
A small black and white street cat
Who isn't sure yet
He just doesn't know
In the defense of graven idols
In the defense of confessed criminals
Who conspire with enemies
Of the state?
Of the people?
I bury my face in newly dried laundry
A northern star
A reminder
Not all nouns wander

Was it 2am or
July when I remembered the mouthful
The mouthful of yellow jackets
A thing I needed to learn about stubbornness
Memory
The accusation
Somewhere between magic and
Alchemy and the dazzle
Drawn from one or another water
That the morals of a time must always be
Decanted
From people who ruled
Rather than those who were stolen
That the sidewalk crack grime
Only flakes from one class of people
And that a thousand songs of transformation
Of the gods of release
Of escape
Are not proof
That morals of a time are somehow
One over rinsed poem
One essay
One speech
Worn once and

Handed down into transformation
The transformation from gold
Into love
A thing we translate from some languages into the word
Survival
A word that will be translated again into
Unworthy
A word that will be used that way until
One wordless healing song
Dressed in a garage sale shirt
Remembers what it used to mean
And maybe someone sits at that table
Reminding you that there is
More than one key to this house
While one speech
Still debates the humanity of thousands

Which bells hammered you into shape?
We've invaded
Portland
In need of a bridge
Brunch
A distraction
The train tracks are singing
The longer this thing goes
The more my scars show
Staring out through a zoom window
Clutching the blade of a
Carbon steel knife in my bare left hand
Like it was nothing
I have lost more than this
Watch them
Watch my scars come up
Come visible
The train tracks are screaming with the weather change
We have invaded Portland
We needed a rare book
One that won't be read
In this light
In this time
I have run to the Multnomah village site

Like a child to home base
Like a child in a game
My scars on display
I touch the pavement
A scar
I touch
A tree old enough to have known
A tree
Humming the possible
I stare
Into the eyes of a bully
Stare from my safe place
Am declared useless for his purposes
Train tracks singing
The cure is a way off
We need ghosts
We have invaded Portland
We have nailed down the train tracks
We are a brutal choreography
We become visible

This wind is the antidote
Momentary
Scaled
Rattling warning
We are working on a net
A knot for each of our dead a
Knot for each stressed and
Poorly chosen word
The unqualified can always be questioned
To the point of collapse
This net we're making
We're hoping to catch ourselves again
This endless numbering of the dead
The relentless year
Collections of a thing that isn't history
But justification
A collection of transgressors
Another warning rattle
These fangs are hinged the words
They are hinged
The history
A police report that doesn't match the footage
The wind rattles
The wind rattles bronze

Brought down hard against the sidewalk
Shattered
Leaving edges
Sharp as disappointment
We don't even know what to call this idea
A broken thing
Finally
Something we are all allowed to share

How many fireworks will it take to drive off the demons
        of our time?
I want to crochet a solution
Write you a solution
I want to take magic
Made of glass
Made of silk
Made of stone
Made of words
And use the tools that I know
To unravel these conjurings of
Entitlement and greed and fear
To make a dust that we can fluff into our feathers to
Kill or drive off the parasites
To prove
Once and for all
That a system that designates murderers
And sets them on its people
Is not sustainable
And it is not working

III

My hero poets are leaving
Not all at once
Not everyone
But too many
Too fast
Too often in these last two years
And here on the day some people called
Summer's end
I was shivering at my kitchen table
I was shivering and watching the storm cloud over
San Bruno Mountain
I was thinking about my hero poets
Danger of poets
Fearless poets
And one of them sent me a poem
Just now
Like a very sharp knife
Between someone else's ribs
I'm not even a little cold anymore

There is an empty part that echoes cold
Echoes cold
I wrap
Garlands of your words
Twined with
Prayers we both learned early
A hand clasp
A belonging
The habit of pulling the stuff of self into words
A habit of words like sacred herbs
Words that taste like
Apricots
Apples
Salt
Songs from those other mountains
One I find myself singing this morning
Today
I may bake the bread of childhood
Light the candles of my grandmothers
Today
And in other times
I will wear the red thread of your words
At my wrist.

for Jack

They didn't give us a day
We pulled it from this resisting calendar
Grandma went back later
Wise and experienced
With a digging stick
To get the root
Just in case
How do we make a day last a year
Now there's a miracle to recut into ceremony
I walk February
May
December afternoons with my pockets full of
October days
One for each of 50 plus years
They whisper to my grandfather
To my dad
My cousins
They whisper
Yes
You were here
You are here
These stories matter

Numbers slide through the fingers
At this end of the year
The twelve become three the
Thirty become three
The wisdom spring under the three roots
I can't keep track of all of the magick
The potions that ease the poem pangs
The blood and honey the
Mythical springs the
Times of wonder the
Cryptids that poets are the
Secret stories of hours between
Hours of transition of
Transforming
Here
In this hour
Fingers on the weaving roots
I struggle to pull poems from an even older promise

Wren boys wander
Rain-stroke
Obscure
Draw around them
Dark feathers
Stir the darkness and
Ask their question
We sing the solstice misluck down
Sing to lure safety
Dance new oaths
Are granted a mouthful of guest bread each
Find bitter
Find sweet
Press palms to the new
Tie knots of knowing
And chant the wrung year to the edges of water

Poems the
Toys I played with the
Crayons the
Cushions of the furniture forts
Hopscotch chalk
Rubberbands of poem
Saved for high jump cords
I am baffled by people who
Don't think that they are taken by poem
Where did you think your language came from?

Pull on a different mountain range
One leg at a time
You time travel in poem
He told me
I've seen you do it
We went relic spotting
More than once
Through the line up of the '53 Dodgers
Before his heart was broken
Before his heart was broken
Memories never sit as neatly in a prong setting
As a heart solitaire
Memories never sit as neatly

This is where the tattered banner hangs
Taken by the freeway weather
Like feet slipping between chill sheets
Like hope
Song
Of no dreams
Have you
Have you heard music
Music that didn't hand you a memory
Feathers in a left hand
Feathers and tremble
Moth against glass
Banner
Wound into the chain link
Wound in wild weaving
Like feet
Sliding over unfinished floorboards
An idea of floorboards
A slow polish
Step and step
Bringing up the grain
Tree life
Written in dark ridges
Dark ridges the night foot cannot read

Have you heard the music
Music that keeps your memory
Is your banner hanging there
Woven into the metal webbing
Over the freeway?

There is a poem I was
Now a viper fang
Delivering poison
A poem I collect pieces of
Small and polished
Fragments
The sharp tip
Still sticky
I was a poem and I can't remember what I was about
These days
Are days
And the First Lady is a movie screen
Not in the way that every First Lady since the one who
was President
But today I have seen everything but
Boris and Natasha
Across her skirts
I found another piece of the dangerous poem
My past life
Right there on her shoulder
By the light of automatic
Blinking headlights
They will fill the days with
Days
With all of the days and the kids who carry

Rifles and the new story about the man he shot
And the footage of him
Punching a girl in the back of the head
Because
I suppose
He wanted to look brave
But I've also been toxic
I just think maybe
Blame the firing pin
Blame the fragments of a self
Loaded into a clip
And panicked into another felony
That now seems open for debate
I spit another piece of an old self into my right hand
And wonder about bullets loaded with prayers
Which may or may not be free speech
And is probably out after curfew but sure isn't
Peaceful protest
It's night again
Here in the confines of
Things we miss and maybe wish for
My list still doesn't include a firearm but
I've graduated from High School
Still
I remember it being stressful

I don't know
You can hunt the sky and the
Strange place you rent that isn't home
Where the inside of the cupboard is
Painted the color of
Despair
The thing you were really looking for
Because some poet looked out the
Window and saw a bad god
In the city's skyline
And another would rather
Be a demon than feed one
And that sense of well-being you feel
Will be called
Delusion
Call it delusion
Make it a pet
It will curl against the backs of your knees at night
And keep you warm
No matter how many times you say
"Down"
"Off"
But secretly you can be pleased
Because some musician was
Depressed about sixty years ago

And this year it's fashionable again
We've always suspected that a
Warm meal and a good book
In an ugly delightful chair
Might be shallow
I for one know that I have terrible taste in movies
That I like airplane paperbacks and potato chips
But there will always be a
Cherished space for someone who can
Identify the bullshit

How many songs
Sung to self
On solitary walks or
Into the open seam of a book
Or played to kittens
Have suffocated or
Bled out
Been silenced by power?
This communication is true
Strange and
Sorrowful
Has been cried into unlit corners
But don't you want to hear
All of the songs?

Breakfast Guests
Down in
Down here
Along the droning streets
This city stores poet thoughts
Tule boat songs
Mourning Cloak paintings
I have tripped over Bob Kaufman
Coded into pavement
Blood of a police beating or maybe a
Phrase with an eggshell curve
In heavy fog while children wander school paths
I have invited Bob to breakfast here or there or
Even in my own kitchen
Depending upon his mood
In this morning comforted with a downing fog
Bob has returned with the cats
Returned from last night when we all
Called him back to this painful and necessary place
Where at least he will no longer be arrested
But I suggest that that pain was the least
And here we sit
On my stairs
In the dripping fog
Reciting Eliot to one another

We poets send each other breath
But at a distance
We should send each other breath
Even now when breath is dangerous
Still
One of the measures of life
That some take for granted
Some want to control
Some are always willing to throw
Other people's bodies at their fears
Real or imagined
But the poets
We send each other light caught in a drop of water
The feeling of the first cool air of dawn
A sadness that folds you to the ground
Breath
Life
In the hope that we can catch it
And send it on

How To Know If Your Word Fort Is A Poem

Some poems are born as poems
Some poems grow out of being poems
Some poems are born in skin
In fur, in bark, in scale, in chitin
And are loved into poemhood
This can happen like lightening
This can happen like tectonic movement
This can be a mass extinction
All poems find their own level
All poems have cell membranes rather than cell walls
If it smells like the center of the universe it
Might be a poem
It might also be breakfast
Some breakfasts are poems
Some poems are edible
Some poems are poison
Some are venom
Wear heavy poem handling gloves to pick them up
Until you are certain
If it smells like your great-grandma's perfume it
Might be a poem
It might play hide and seek with your nose like violets
Or coat the vestibule of your memory
Like the scent of the dead rat

Behind the washing machine
Fly larva arranged in a hexagon in its open mouth
Which is to say "I will never forget you" can also be a
Prayer of forgetting
Sometimes a word fort should become a ruin
In order to be a poem
Sometimes a word fort is a poem when built and a
Different poem after the siege
Some poems are caught in snares
Some in pit traps
Some you must sneak up on with a fish fork after 4am
Corner them
Then bribe them with leftover holiday candy
Some poems like salted licorice
Some think it tastes like roofing tar
Some like the taste of roofing tar
But to really know if your word fort is a poem
Call to it
Respectfully
As a poem is called
And if it answers
It's a poem

Hunting in the Downtown

You know how the deer on Market Street are
With their stoplight eyes
Picking their way down the old runoff paths
Past the disappearing relocated Indigenous women
The ravens are here to sing us visible
Drumming on their collection of upended pots and
Industrial buckets
Don't you tell me how we've changed
We were right there
Near the department store
Near the burial sites
Singing to the ancestors
This isn't an abstract gesture
It's not a schoolroom exercise
There are predators here
And the maps of safe passage change every day
And the wind comes up in the afternoon
Don't you tell me how we've changed
The roots of this hill have learned what to call us
Just about
Our clothes collected for the festival
Our family members taken to who knows
You might just sit down and listen for a change
I'm not part of your curriculum

We're a whole other thing
Light reflecting off of the miles of glass
How many feet deep was it
Can you hear the water like shattered windows
Piled just like them
Just there where the tall buildings lean like stealing

Is that prayer smoke
Smeared like fingerprints
Inexpertly lifted
As we stalk the edges of September the
Hint of September
No one told her she isn't the seventh anymore
It takes awhile to recognize the changes
There won't be a quiz at the end of the week
Not here
Our hands full of
Word fish
See how they flash in the hand
In the fingertip's eye
See how they flash and call the water
Is that fog or smoke?
The crow asks me from a tenuous perch on power lines
Is that fog?
Can I have one of those cashews?
I leave one on the windowsill
Something rides the air down the street
Something else
California is praying in panic
In the smoke of house fires and hillsides
You can always be part of the mix
As long as it's the part chosen by someone else
Is that fog?

The folded city finds August most clearly
Just before dawn
Pin striped tuxedo cat and the
Sunday paper
Then the gradual dawn through
San Bruno Mountain fog
Gift peaches
Lunch
Under the loquat tree
City unfolding in sharp
Short flashes
Like a map
Like a leaf
Like a poison flower
A medicine flower
Like patience
The tide of strangers all unaware
Not everyone new is a stranger
The city
Folded for the moment
Purrs
Forepaws kneading the sidewalk

The city forest isn't a sculpture
It is a
Sculpture
Self-assembling and
Falling apart and
Taken apart and
Sold at a distance and
Used as symbol a machine
A meat grinder
A sidewalk household
Facades that tell stories from other times and the
New stories that carry no weight of symbol at all
Some
But not all
Are neighbors and
The sculpture is unquiet
The clicking and
Quiet singing runs all the way through all hours
And visionaries have developed a way of telling the
future
By reading the lights in the windows on this hillside
Sing to me louder
I will love you forever like the
Strange whimsy that wanders these hills with the
Model train sets and the

Secret belief in genocide hand in hand with
Commerce
The threat the
Threat of an untied rope
A rope made of braids cut from mocked men and
Women stolen from themselves
Stolen from the hills
With the gold and that
Comforting smell of sun warmed wildflowers
And hidden water and
Hiding water and
Objects resentfully renamed
The city isn't a sculpture
It's a sculpture
The only perpetual motion machine that works
Heartbroken and smug and
Struggling in
Joy and
Knowing that it's important to pick a side
A face of the polyhedron
Perched on toes by the
Pacific
Say the names of the villages that were
The lakes that are and the lakes that
Curl wishing under the schools and

Old churches
Along with the salamanders and the
Bunch grass
Say the names of the toes of the shoeless
Who lick this peninsula into a mammal
A sculpture
The misdrawn and
Misunderstood coastal sage and the
Quiet overlooked bats
This city isn't a sculpture
The walls rebarred with bones
Bones of stickleback and
Hopeful invasion
The city is self-aware the city is a
Sculpture the city
Is afraid of inconsequence of
Ghost ships that soak in a memory of the bay
Of hillsides that seep in the wet months
Of stands of trees and the latest
Import plants
The city crawls with intention and
Coyotes and
Coydogs and
Lapdogs and
Rats that feed on excellent garbage
The city isn't a sculpture

These are the stones whose names I've forgotten
The one I have been using for a right eye
It's in shades of light brown and grey
And is frighteningly accurate when looking at
Songbirds
And fugitive political hostilities
Another stone panics for me because
I don't have time anymore
It's blue
This one looks like marble
Luminous as skin
It's too heavy to be marble
It might be marble
It might be cursed skin
I write with a soft
Warm
Stone
But can never be sure what words will come out
This transparent stone has been scanning the
Prophecies
She is trying to tell me something

Western gull reports the weather from the
Farallons
Sounds like
Schoolyard lunch
The way the weather does sometimes
Walking the Great Highway in blowing rain
Ravens
Ravens and
Magical sand
Beak clicks
Clicks
Folksong
Sometimes at street level
Sometimes
The way that weather does

A Prayer for Tonga

From here we watch the surf
Examine the sky for songs of Tonga
In the bay the water breathes
Altered
A word
Another
Rose sky at dusk
More news
We are on hearts edge for you
Cousins
We choose and send our best prayers of safety
A promise of help
When help is possible

Planetrise
Roofsitting
Just outside the bedroom window
Telling the future by
Lights coming on
Lights on the mountain
Roof board
Sunwarm
Weather this year is
Storm
Taste
Storm
Neighbor cat
Stare
Roof poet
Yard rummage
Planetrise
Doors of the year
Creak
But the hinges hold

Today arrives on all four feet
Balanced
In a drizzly fog
Street cat tells me secrets
Shyly and one at a time
Rain holds the sand down
Holds the sand until it can dry it
Can lift it
To blow like mystery a foot above the beach
Raven clacks
Mumbles
Blown rain
Blown cold
Like mystery
Just like it

Before Dawn
Waterfalls wait
Rocks
Loose on the faces
Yearn for sea level
Twigs
Caught in iced puddles
All on toe tip
After Sunrise
Road clings to rock
To tree root
Glittering dangerously
This hillside
That one
On the move
Water
Released
Sings down

I guess that I write about stars
At the end of December
Even though most are planets
And I have no idea what they call themselves
Hard to navigate with the unfixed
When unfixed
Just all keeping up with traffic
They use the word interrogate
But I've never questioned that light
Any more than the others I can see
On San Bruno Mountain
We just sing together
In pitchy delight
And only sometimes wonder where
Or when
We are

The sacred in the day can be difficult
Can require excavation
The birds and I aren't sure
Thumb tip between the eyebrows
Twenty-seven crows arranged in asymmetry
Twenty-eight of us watching
Sun up and the attendant
Brief
Distractions
We scatter
Hunting the rest of morning
Hunting the sacred
One of us will find it
Our beaks will poke and pry until we do
Some days require prying

Dark whispers late in these days
Between solstice and someone's new year
Rain
Gossip against the window glass
Prying at the frame
Picking with cold sharp fingers
Year spins in
Spins out the
Year
These rearrangings these
Levels
We lose gravity
We fall
Are caught
We fall and land
We fall
We're still falling

Morning is best to bake the milk and honey bread
Conjuring of simple expectations
Poppy seed cake wants a different hour
Sauteed mushrooms
Simple touches of the other world
Aching and unavoidable
Apples, prunes and walnuts for protection
Beet and cabbage soup
Promise of healing
Fish
Herbs from the creek
The water is also generous
Beans and peas
Two hands full of barley
A cut pear
For abundance

Odin's hunt arrives early in
Wind and hail
Guest cats
Dark fluff
Share breakfast on the porch
And all of the glitter and flicker of
Candles
Of warm
Heart leap of this weather, this
Weather in the darkness
We break the barriers of salt and
Scatter
Star sand
Magnetite
We scatter all of the warm herbs at the threshold
On the sills
Scatter cinnamon on the cut apples
And leave the predictive stones in their bag
The near soon can keep the secrets
In this home
There is mystery enough

Rain memory
Returns to scream
To whisper
Identity
To the wood and glass
Wood
Glass
In this season of fire
Nights shake themselves
Dance careful passes
According to the traditions that they know
Wind
Rain
Wishes unpicked
Will shatter into rubies
Rubies to shell danger
Emeralds for patience
Rain
Panting against the walls
One
Beeswax candle
Remembering
In a lean hour
Remembering a different math

In January we roll in stars
All cold and edges and the hope of feeling
Dance the moon of cold
Sing wet days
Sharpened again
Into the narrow end of the arbitrary decision of year
Make ink from the grounds of medicine we have taken
Thread a needle we will call reclaiming
And pull the cut edges of this place
Close enough to stitch

Bell calls
Banishes
Third day of the new sun
Ghosts of the season
Clinging to washed spoon
Peering into the mixing bowl
Spice can ring like a bell too
In these crowded and grasping days
Mother's night
Plans her sacrifice
Her preservation
Wanders the wooden floors in
Grain
Against grain
Where the wood eddies and pools
Ghosts of the season
Small and waning reverberations
Pick garnets to sleep in
Curl and uncurl in practice
This breathing house
Crowded with old things
Things draped in last year's flowers
Blown eggs
And careful
Practice

Ghost creeks
Particularly loud today
Sound twisting the fog
In the aftermath of another
Firework night
This year a battlefield
The music of it
The death of it
Some mornings we are past blame
Past singing of our own
Just dragging our chosen mysteries
To the next
Killing ground

In this time
The rivers shifting
The language changing
As every language must
And the wind comes on to the shore
And it frays the cloud edges
And muddles our thoughts in the afternoon
This week
We're hip deep in redefinition
Stare into the face of the past
Stare into our pain and our loss
And our fairytale
The one we mistakenly made our heart out of
Then left the hotel room without it
So now
We pull the wind into the hole where our hearts were
Imagining that we need something
Inside us
So we can keep our balance
But wind shifts and rummages leaving us feeling
Uncertain

Speckled feather caught in a spider's web
Caught in a spider's web as the wind rises
I have twined and unpicked my ropes
So many times
My back to the mast of a ship that changes
My ship keeps changing shape
Keeps
Pressing the pulse of wind
Like a poet looking for a rule to break
When some of us look like window glass
We look like
A bell
Like a wind
That doesn't know it's the wind
Now that spider's web is full of wings
That catch the downing sun
Catch fire
Catch night coming
Catch a thought in the crow's eye
And twist and unpick
From the point of contact
The rule
Like one of those poets

Dancing backwards
Wing walking
Finding absolution
One feather at a time

Kim Shuck is the 7th Poet Laureate Emerita of San Francisco. Shuck is author of ten books of poems and prose. She is also editor, co-editor, part of the editing team or edit curious for ten anthologies. Kim has various awards and fellowships associated with her writing ranging from a Inaugural National Laureate Fellowship and a Censorship Award from PEN Oakland to a Second Place in a radio screenplay contest in 6th grade.

Pick a Garnet to Sleep in is set in Joanna Nova Book and Scala Jewel Pro.